FRAN HODGKINS

THE SECRET
GALAXY

Photographs by Mike Taylor

A TILBURY HOUSE NATURE BOOK

Seeing Stars

The light from homes, offices, stores, vehicles, and street lamps can make stars hard to see at night. This is called light pollution.

Seeing stars is easier where (or when) there are fewer lights. If you go stargazing, give your eyes a few minutes to get used to the dark.

· ·

Put together from many separate nighttime satellite photos, this image shows lights on Earth's surface. The most urbanized areas glow the brightest, while areas such as deep jungle, tundra, and desert show few lights.

You might not know I'm here.
Sunlight hides me by day,
and at night the city lights dazzle your eyes.
But if you look when the night is deep...

You'll see me stretched across the sky
from horizon to horizon.
The ancient Greeks named me the Milky Way,
because to them I looked like
milk spilled in the night sky.
Their word for "milk" became
the word galaxy.
I am the Milky Way galaxy.

The Milky Way

The Milky Way galaxy is a huge disk-shaped spiral, and Earth, the sun, and the other planets of our solar system are on one arm. When we look toward the center of our vast galaxy, we see the glowing ribbon of stars we call the Milky Way. All the stars we can see distinctly in the night sky—within the milky ribbon and outside it—are in our galaxy, and some of these make up constellations such as Orion and the Big Bear.

. . . .

In places without light pollution, the Milky Way is the most noticeable feature in the night sky. It looks like a wide ribbon of stars.

Moving Fast While Sitting Still

Think you're sitting still while reading? Guess again. In the time it takes to read this sentence, you have moved nearly two miles (3.2 km) due to Earth's rotation alone. And at the same time, Earth is going around the sun at nearly 67,000 miles per hour and our solar system is moving around the galaxy's center at 490,000 miles every hour. If you could run that fast, you could go from New York to Los Angeles in 20 seconds!

Dizzy yet?

Even though the Milky Way galaxy is spinning so fast, it takes about 225 million years to complete a rotation. One revolution ago, dinosaurs were just beginning to roam Earth.

. . . .

This artist's rendering shows what the Milky Way galaxy would look like if we could see it from above the disk.

I whirl in a spiral with my starry arms trailing.
You and Earth and your sun and solar system
are on one arm, but don't worry.
Gravity holds everything together.
No stars get left behind.

Sun

A Lot of Zeroes!

One hundred billion is a 1 followed by 11 zeroes. How big a number is that? Just one billion grains of sand would fill a dump truck. You would need 100 trucks to hold a hundred billion grains of sand.

Your sun is only one of my 200 billion stars,
and there are 100 billion other galaxies like me in the visible universe.
Your ancestors have watched me from the dawn of history,
but I don't give up my secrets easily.

As Earth rotates, the Milky Way seems to rise in the east and move westward across the sky.

Not everyone thought of milk when they looked at me.
In China I was called the Silver River.
Scandinavians called me Vintergaten, their word for winter road,
and the Thai used the name
"Path of the White Elephant."

Time Traveling With Just a Look

When you look up into the sky, you're really looking back in time. You aren't seeing the stars as they are, but as they used to be. There may be billions of stars and galaxies out there that we can't see, because they are so far away their light hasn't reached us yet.

Light moves incredibly fast—more than 670,000,000 miles an hour. If you could move that fast, in just one second you could circle the Earth seven and a half times! But even at that speed, light from other stars takes a very long time to reach us. On the picture of the Milky Way shown earlier, you wouldn't be able to tell the sun from Proxima Centauri, the star closest to us. However, light from that star travels more than four years before it reaches Earth. That's how far away the stars are.

Nothing is really as it seems in this photo because the stars may actually have changed since the light that we see left them. Some may no longer exist.

The Algonquin viewed me as the path of departed warriors,
and the Micmac said I was made of firebirds.
To the Cherokee I was corn meal scattered by a naughty dog.
Bad dog!

Secrets of the Aurora

If you live in northern lands, you may see the Milky Way behind the aurora borealis, or northern lights, which are not part of the galaxy. Northern lights form in the upper regions of Earth's atmosphere when particles from the sun interact with Earth's magnetic field. Expanding, contracting, red or green, ghostly or intense, northern lights are an awe–inspiring sight. The Inuit people said the lights were a result of a ball game between people or perhaps even between walruses.

The northern lights glow brightly against the backdrop of stars in this photo taken at Pemaquid Point, Maine.

Time Passages

For much of human history, Earth was believed to be the center of the universe, with the sun, planets, and stars in orbit around it. The first people who challenged this belief suffered for their ideas, sentenced to prison or even death. Today's astronomers stand on the shoulders of pioneering scientists as they learn more about the universe.

What am I really?

I am neither milk nor corn meal, nor birds nor roads,

though you could say that I've given birth to all those things.

I am made of dust, gas, stars, and star stuff.

The wonders of Earth and the sky come together in this photo of the Milky Way and the Corona Arch, located just outside Moab, Utah. Although millions of years old, Corona Arch is still much younger than the galaxy.

Stars are born in giant clouds of gas and dust.
They live billions of years—maybe longer.
Since the universe began, 14 billion years have passed.
I've been around for 12 billion of those years.
I've seen stars born, live, and die.

B

A

A Starry Nursery

If conditions are right, dust and gas collapse, condense, and become a star. New stars are born in great clouds of gas and dust called nebulas.

Stars glow in different colors because they are different temperatures. The hottest, most intense stars glow blue. Moderately hot stars like our sun are yellow. Cooler stars are usually red.

There is a lot of dust in the galaxy. So much dust, in fact, that we can't see everything even with our most powerful telescopes. Scientists use other wavelengths of energy, such as radio waves and infrared—to see. Unlike visible light, those wavelengths aren't blocked by dust.

Stars are near birth and near death in this image of a giant nebula. Newborn stars will soon emerge from the bright pillar of gas and dust at A. The bright blue star at B will soon explode into a supernova.

It's Elementary

Carbon, oxygen, and nitrogen are three elements that are essential to life on Earth. Without them, life as we know it—including this ancient tree in the desert and you—would not exist. As the astronomer Carl Sagan said, "We are star-stuff."

. . . .

This tree is in Dead Horse Canyon State Park in Utah.

Earth and all the planets are made of the stuff of stars,
and most of the atoms of every living thing were born in a star.
Carbon, oxygen, nitrogen—almost everything that is in you—
was forged inside a star long ago.

The Death of a Star

Stars like the sun glow because deep within their cores, atoms are being fused together into new, larger atoms. Hydrogen atoms become helium atoms. This fusion releases a huge amount of energy. We experience this energy from the sun as heat and light.

Fusion goes on until all the hydrogen in a star's core has been fused into helium. What happens next depends on the star's mass. Mass is the amount of matter contained in an object.

The Butterfly Nebula is the remnant of a star.

Within each star, atoms fuse,
building element after element.
When fusion stops, the core implodes and releases
a lot of energy that blows apart the star,
and all the atoms there zoom outward into space,
becoming the building blocks of everything.

For a star, mass means everything.
The more massive a star, the hotter it burns,
and the shorter its life.
A star like the sun ends as a white dwarf.
A more massive star ends as a neutron star.
The most massive stars become black holes.

When is a star not a star? When it's a shooting star. These streaks of light, called meteors, are actually small bits of dirt or rock that burn up in Earth's atmosphere.

A Star's Fate

Space may look empty, but it's not. The space between the stars is actually rich in elements such as carbon, nitrogen, and oxygen that were ejected from earlier generations of stars. Ultimately, the material from past generations of stars becomes part of new stars.

Seeing Indirectly

Although they can't be seen, black holes give themselves away. A stellar black hole will affect the movement of objects nearby. It may make gas and dust around it move very quickly and give off X-rays and other forms of radiation that belie the black hole's presence.

In this artist's conception, a black hole's powerful gravity tears away gas from a nearby star.

Light can't escape from a black hole,
and matter doesn't stand a chance.
Black holes suck up gas, dust, and stars.
What happens inside a black hole?
That's another secret.

At the Heart of the Galaxy

The black hole at the center of the Milky Way is called Sagittarius A–star (or Sgr A* for short). Supermassive black holes may be at the center of every galaxy. These black holes are far more massive than the sun, but pack that mass into a comparatively small space. As a result, supermassive black holes have unbelievably strong gravity. They pull in the stars and gas near the center of the galaxy, growing even more massive as they do.

. . . .

An artist created this image based on what scientists know about supermassive black holes. At the edge of the black hole, a place called the event horizon, time and reality may be quite different from what we know.

A black hole lives at my heart, too,
but it's different from one formed by a star.
My black hole has the mass of four million suns,
yet it could fit inside Earth's orbit around the sun.

I'm not only stars and planets,
    but also the mysterious, guessed-at stuff in between that
        makes up the me you can't see.
Most of me is made up of dark matter and dark energy.
    What are these things, exactly?
        That's a secret I'm keeping, for now.

So Much Unseen

Matter is anything that takes up space and has mass. Scientists think there is more to the universe than can be seen. They call this invisible material "dark matter." Dark matter and dark energy make up about 96 percent of the universe, based on observation of gravity's effects on visible matter. Of what's left, a quarter is the bright stuff that makes up stars. The rest is gas that stretches between galaxies.

. . . .

In this artist's rendition, the dark blue areas show where dark matter would have to be to cause the distortion of distant galaxies that astronomers have observed.

All of us—
stars, black holes, you and me, and naughty dogs—
are on the move as the universe expands and we galaxies move apart.
What will happen next?
That's the biggest secret of all.

The Milky Way arches over a
stand of trees in Maine.

What Happens Next?

Astronomers discovered that the universe is getting bigger faster and faster. What will happen in billions of years? We don't know for sure. Perhaps you will solve the riddle.

Photo credits
2–3 NASA/Goddard Space Flight Center Scientific Visualization Studio; 6-7 NASA, ESA, and The Hubble Heritage Team (STScI/Aura)/Acknowledgment: P. Knezek (WIYN); 16–17 Wolfgang Brandner (JPL/IPAC), Eva K. Grebel (Univ. Washington), You-Hua Chu (Univ. Illinois Urbana-Champaign), and NASA; 20-21 NASA, ESA, and the Hubble SM4 ERO Team; 24–25 ESA, NASA and Felix Mirabel; 26-27 NASA/JPL-Caltech; 28–29 NASA, ESA, M.J. Jee and H. Ford (Johns Hopkins Univ.); **all others** Mike Taylor

Tilbury House, Publishers
12 Starr St.
Thomaston, Maine 04861
800-582-1899 • www.tilburyhouse.com

Dedications
For the wonderful people at the RPL and TH, and to Kathy S., with many thanks. —FH
Dedicated to my parents and my sister, who always encouraged me to chase my dreams; to the International Dark-Sky Association, as they continue to raise public awareness about light pollution; and to the young astronomers among us who will help us learn so much more about our place in the cosmos. —MT

First hardcover edition October 2014 • 10 9 8 7 6 5 4 3 2 1

ISBN 978-0-88448-391-5

Library of Congress Cataloging-in-Publication Data

Hodgkins, Fran, 1964– author.
  The secret galaxy / Fran Hodgkins; photographs by Mike Taylor. —First hardcover edition.
      pages cm
  Summary: "When you gaze into the sky at night, what do you see? Most of us see only the brightest stars because they are the only ones that can cut through the artificial light that overwhelms the night. But up there, beyond the haze of streetlights and buildings, lies the Milky Way--our home galaxy. The words and photos in The Secret Galaxy allow young readers to see the stars as never before."—Provided by publisher.

  ISBN 978-0-88448-391-5
  1. Milky Way—Juvenile literature. I. Taylor, Mike (Michael Thomas), 1973- illustrator. II. Title.
  QB857.7.H63 2014
  523.1'13—dc23
                                                        2014014083

Book design by Bumblecat Design & Illustration; jacket design by Ann Casady
Printed by Worzalla, Stevens Point, WI.

Scan the code to visit
the Tilbury Learning Center.